Add-Verse to Presidents

"To Larry from Mark"

Taylor Jones

ADD~VERSE TO PRESIDENTS

by TAYLOR JONES

Dembner Books

NEW YORK

Dembner Books
Published by Red Dembner Enterprises Corp.
1841 Broadway, New York, N.Y. 10023
Distributed by W. W. Norton & Company, Inc.
500 Fifth Avenue, New York, N.Y. 10110

Library of Congress Cataloging in Publication Data

Jones, Taylor.
    Add-verse to presidents.

    1.   Presidents—United States—Caricatures and cartoons.
2.   American wit and humor, Pictorial.   I.   Title.
E176.1.J66   973'.09'92   81-17391
ISBN 0-934878-09-9 (pbk.)   AACR2

To Giles Inman
Ty Ty, Georgia

Contents

Foreword

Great talent comes across an editor's door in many guises.

For me, it appeared in the middle 1970s in the person of a youngster who looked to be about thirteen and claimed to be a cartoonist-caricaturist.

His name was Taylor Jones, his college was Cornell (in Iowa, not Ithaca), and his ability to capture a subject on the end of his pen and pencil and make it wiggle was staggering.

Rising to the opportunity, while ever mindful of my obligation to my fellow stockholders in our newspaper, the *Delta Democrat-Times* of Greenville, Mississippi, I offered him a sweetheart of a deal.

He could work for us during the summer, "gaining valuable experience" as the expression went, and we would print whatever we liked of what he produced and pay him the minimum wage.

Whether he was overpaid or underpaid is not a subject for debate. Speaking as one party to the deal, I can testify that the *Democrat-Times* got the best bargain since Thomas Jefferson pulled off the Louisiana Purchase.

Whether many of the presidents, living and dead, whom Taylor Jones has spitted in word and line on the following pages would thank me for my shrewd prescience is doubtful. Jefferson, for instance, might gladly return the Louisiana Territory if Taylor would withdraw his likeness from this collection.

On one question there can be little doubt. Without regard to age, Taylor Jones is one of the most gifted practitioners of his art form, bringing acute vision and imaginative distortion to the men and women he delineates on paper. To see his presidents parade before us is never to be able to see them in the same old way again.

Happily for me, Taylor has had to admit one real failure over the past decade or so. He never could do a satisfactory editorial portrait of me, which may explain so readily why I accepted the invitation to write this preface.

But I would like to believe that even if he had managed to pin me to the page along with his other subjects, I would have been able to admire his artistic candor. In laying bare that which the public men and women he portrays would rather minimize or obscure, he performs a vital public service. God save us all when the day comes that editorial cartoonists flatter their victims and conceal their warts. As long as Taylor Jones is around, we need not fear that day's arrival.

Hodding Carter III
Former Assistant Secretary of State

Add-Verse to Presidents

George Washington   **1789-1797**

Proper oral hygiene, it must be understood
Is difficult at best with teeth made of wood

Oh a grim rinse, indeed, if one brushes with shellac
And it's tough to floss termites from molars way back

So when the frontier dentist made his spring round
The Father of our Country could nowhere be found

"Anything, please, but spare me plier, plane, and drill
In the forests next Mount Vernon, I'll seek an ivory-bill"

Now dentistry today's much improved, don't you think?
Lucky, too, since the ivory-bill's likely extinct

Add-Monitions, footnotes to presidential history, begin on page 91

John Adams   1797-1801

"Dear Peach," Adams wrote, to his wife Abigail
"My enemies take me for some species of whale

They jeer, 'His Rotundity'—they're horribly vicious
And what the newspapers say, I'd call it seditious!

'Blind, bald, toothless, querulous,' snaps one editor
Such cruel observations, though I'll grant three of four"

"Dear Plum," replied Abby, while sipping her tea
"The problem's as simple as X, Y and Z

The reason some folks find you loathsome and vile
Is you gobble down meals like a starved crocodile

Now chew mutton thoroughly and avoid spiced beef
Please limit the baked beans—give us all some relief!"

Thomas Jefferson   1801-1809

Be it Barbary pirates or embargo to ponder
The elegant man's fickle mind would soon wander

Far from the mud streets and mosquitos of Washington
Safe from the intrigues of A. Burr and Al Hamilton

To the place where he bloomed an engaging fellow
Speaking, of course, of his beloved Monticello

There he could tend to great matters of state
Like indexing the flora upon his estate

With servants at breakfast it wouldn't be odd
To find him debating the meaning of God

Or later, still clad in but bathrobe and slippers
Consorting with Sally over fried chicken livers

James Madison   **1809-1817**

Little "Jemmy" Madison scarcely was able
To sit back in a chair and still reach the table

Yet he managed, somehow, quill clasped with both hands
To draft a Constitution that, somehow, still stands

James Monroe   1817-1825

It was practically dizzy with wheelings and dealings
That so-called "Era of Very Good Feelings"

Whatever else could have given rise
To the lamented Missouri Compromise?

Marbury vs. Madison? No, that came before
Washington Irving? No, he was an author

You can see now, alas, the jam that we're in
Nothing rhymes rightly with Monroe's Doctrine

John Quincy Adams   1825-1829

Best mark our words, Jacksonians say
His blood flows cold as Hudson Bay

He forged a deal with Henry Clay
And robbed us on Election Day

Best watch your step; best keep aware
Lest he catch you in his icy stare

But we'll get him back; Old Hickory'll take care
And we'll feed John Q. to a polar bear

Andrew Jackson   **1829-1837**

Old Hickory, a fighter, a saint to the debtor
Democracy unleashed, Common Man he unfettered

And nothing made Andy more irate
Than the Second Bank of the United States

He vetoed its charter, and Congress sustained him
Not pleased with just that, Hickory moved on a whim:

He grabbed his spittoon and filled it with spittle
Then mailed the receptacle to Nicholas Biddle

The banker on opening the package recoils
Engraved on the urn: "To the victor, the spoils"

Martin Van Buren   1837-1841

The reign of Old Hickory proved a tough act to follow
For the little red Dutchman from up Sleepy Hollow

Though a master politico, nicknamed the "Red Fox"
As president, Van Buren straight away hit the rocks

In 1837, a depression there came
But the voters, of course, held Van Buren to blame

William Henry Harrison   1841

After all that hoopla for Tippecanoe
You'd think he'd have had something better to do

Than make his inaugural, minus hat, coat or tails
Old fool: one month later—as dead as doornails!

John Tyler   1841-1845

It was "Tyler Too" who set precedent
By which the veep becomes president

The Constitution was quite obscure
On law concerning this procedure

But after the death of Tippecanoe
John Tyler showed them who was who

He vetoed Whig programs right and left
Leaving the Whig party quite bereft

Henry Clay was so mad he could have spat
Harrison's veep was—a Democrat!

James K. Polk   **1845-1849**

The Dark Horse Candidate James K. Who?
Amazing, what he managed to do

Made promises in the campaign that fall
Then somehow he managed to keep them all

Revised the tariff, urged independent treasury
Acquired California, settled Oregon's boundary

Old pols keep promising, but that's enough said
Let's bring James Polk right back from the dead

Zachary Taylor   1849-1850

With "manifest destiny" calling the orders
Disputing so boldly those Texas borders

America staged itself a show
That kindled a war with Mexico

General Taylor's soldiers sang by rumor
"From the Halls of Montezuma"

While proud Buena Vista fell
On "To the Stores of Taco Bell"

Millard Fillmore   **1850-1853**

Dear Millard, oh Millard, what did you do?
Must history credit nothing to you?

You're mentioned in one book, but barely that
It says that at midnight you put out the cat

Franklin Pierce   **1853-1857**

Oh how unruly Franklin's hair did grow
In Sectional tangles, as the winds blow

The Kansas-Nebraska Act snarled in his mats
While John Brown engaged in violent spats

Frank's scalp got so strained, it made him wince
It's clear he needed a thorough cream rinse

James Buchanan   1857-1861

It's not me they're after, let that much be said
But the High Court's decision on Scott they dread

Now as to who'll be slave and who'll be free
I doubt that the answer should come from me

Our grand Constitution has got me to thinkin'
Why not pass this question along to Abe Lincoln?

Abraham Lincoln   1861-1865

The tintypes are thoroughly fixed in our minds
His somber face solidly etched with dark lines

It speaks for a nation unhallowed, at war
But with it sure hope to unite it once more

The eyes, though grave, seem to radiate light
Sleepless, they gaze down the hallway at night

Mouth's a bit crooked; top lip stretches a while
How hard to imagine in the shape of a smile

Andrew Johnson   1865-1869

All through the roll call, while Congress impeaches
Andrew Johnson awaits, while mending old breeches

Some Republicans, determined to be the South's jailor
Balk at Reconstruction by a Tennessee tailor

Senate radicals plotted, but despite all prediction
Mr. Johnson got off, one vote shy of conviction

Ulysses S. Grant   1869-1877

See the hero of Vicksburg, chomping cigars
See the dying old man, penning memoirs

To his regime the label of "scandal!" was pinned
That's our picture of Grant, three sheets to the wind

Rutherford B. Hayes   1877-1881

Carpetbaggers, Boss Tweed and Reconstruction
Marred the Centennial of our war-torn nation

Reckon Grant's booze, plus electoral scandal
It was more than weary voters could handle

So Hayes kept his word: Union troops were withdrawn
While the First Lady served lemonade on the lawn

James A. Garfield   1881

When Garfield grew tired of partisan struggling
He'd humor himself with odd stunts or juggling

For ignoring the Spoils System, his term was cut short
He was shot in the back by a crazed party stalwart

Chester Alan Arthur   1881-1885

Now President Arthur set a most royal routine
Rising late in the morning, then only to preen

To his warm bubble bath he'd add a gallon of milk
Then doff his pyjamas, which were sewed of fine silk

For an hour after bathing he'd fuss with his hair
Before giving thought to descending the stair

On a brunch of poached quail's eggs King Arthur would fatten
Then loll through the p.m. in French furs and satin

. . . But as for those muttonchops, it's often been said
He trained White House squirrels to perch on his head

Grover Cleveland   1885-1889; 1893-1897

As president Grover Cleveland's biggest wish
Was to spend his mornings dining on fish

The reform-minded bachelor had a distaste
For White House style cooking and government waste

Down at the wharf he'd bark loud for herring
He never minded that people were staring

Some thought his bachelorhood quite unwholesome
So at last he up and married Miss Folsom

And survived as our only non-consecutive
Herring-loving Chief Executive

Benjamin Harrison   1889-1893

List his accomplishments; there must be a few
Besides being the grandson of Tippecanoe

Here's one: a treaty citing Hawaii all through it
But President Cleveland later withdrew it

Sometimes a strand of beard fell from his face
Aside from that, Old Ben left nary a trace

William McKinley   **1897-1901**

McKinley closed out the Gilded Age
History books turned an imperial page

For overseas islands we'd developed a thirst
Our mouths made to water by Randolph Hearst

God spoke to McKinley; He told him, "Havana!
My blessings upon thee and Marcus A. Hanna"

McKinley sang praises, rising up from the dust
"God bless America! In Standard Oil we trust!"

Theodore Roosevelt   1901-1909

At Sagamore Hill, twixt antelope and anteaters
Stand, shot and stuffed, several corporate leaders

All trophies attest to the skill of one hunter
A man who, like Zeus, throttled foes with his thunder

Half bull moose, half elephant, hero of San Juan
Shades of Bismarck, Sheriff Dillon and perhaps Genghis Khan

With facets of Byron, Charles Darwin, John Muir
For Americans the mix had pearl-handled allure

William Howard Taft   1909-1913

For Teddy's hard-luck successor, try as he might
The big stick and safari hat didn't feel right

But pursued by a Bull Moose just what could he do
Save escape to the bathroom for a soak and shampoo

So Taft locked the bath door, but there was the rub
All four hundred pounds of him got stuck in the tub

Woodrow Wilson   **1913-1921**

Professor Wilson made it a prime vocation
That the U.S. should join the League of Nations

He'd tour the country up and down
He'd teach Fourteen Points to farm and town

"America First!" the citizens yelled
And by their rejection Wilson was felled

He suffered a stroke, took straight to his bed
By his wife Edith the country was led

League f Nations
Four points :
1. op venants oper
2. fr of seas in pe
3. th oval of econ
4. th uction of arm
5. a nent of
ssia
TJ

Warren G. Harding   1921-1923

First Lady Florence stalks the halls in a huff
She collars a servant: "Enough is enough!

Tell me right now where's that no-good lout
Or you'll be fired—I'll kick you right out!"

In fear the servant points to a closet
"Why there?" Flossy grills. "Well . . . to make a deposit"

Snapping "We'll see about that," she yanks open the door
The president pants, "Here's that hat you're looking for"

Grabbing the cloche, she stares straight in his eye:
"The Ambassador's waiting. Zip up your fly!"

Calvin Coolidge   1923-1929

When asked to give his thought for the day
Cal Coolidge simply walked away

Herbert Hoover   **1929-1933**

"Stand upright for Hoover; would you rather be adrift
On a sea of Irish whiskey, captained by Al Smith?"

So the voters picked Hoover, his garage and his chickens
And one year later it was mighty slim pickin's

Franklin D. Roosevelt   1933-1945

"If you are suffering from Depression or croup
Why not try a warm cup of my alphabet soup?"

"Or if you've contracted unemployment disease
Take a soup injection, dosage ten CCC's"

Here's a letter from the Dust Bowl, written by two men:
"Thanks to your soup, skies above are clear again"

Republican sends cheer from her home in Walla Walla
"Nation's goin' to the dogs, but you're a tough act to Fala"

Harry S. Truman   1945-1953

Harry S. Truman was having a ball
Playing piano for Miss Lauren Bacall

When a reporter queried MacArthur's defiance
Harry pondered the keys for a moment of silence

Said the man from Missouri in a voice crisp and high
"My thoughts of the general are inscribed on my tie"

Dwight Eisenhower   1953-1961

Tell me, Father, just what was it like
Growing up in those days of Ike?

Well, we had mom and pop and good hard work
Maybe a little bebop, and soda jerks

I recollect Fats Domino and Foster Dulles
Edward R. Murrow and, uh, Dobie Gillis

Seems Joe McCarthy hogged the news
And kids were wearing saddle shoes

Remember somethin' about seats on a bus
. . . But you know that lady wasn't one of us

Oh, some funny guys in sweatshirts and sneakers
Nixon gave a speech about his dog—Checkers

Elvis Presley sang about hound dogs, with pelvic kinks
And Ike? He was occasionally seen on the links

Anything else, son, that you want to know?
No, Dad, I think I'll let the subject go

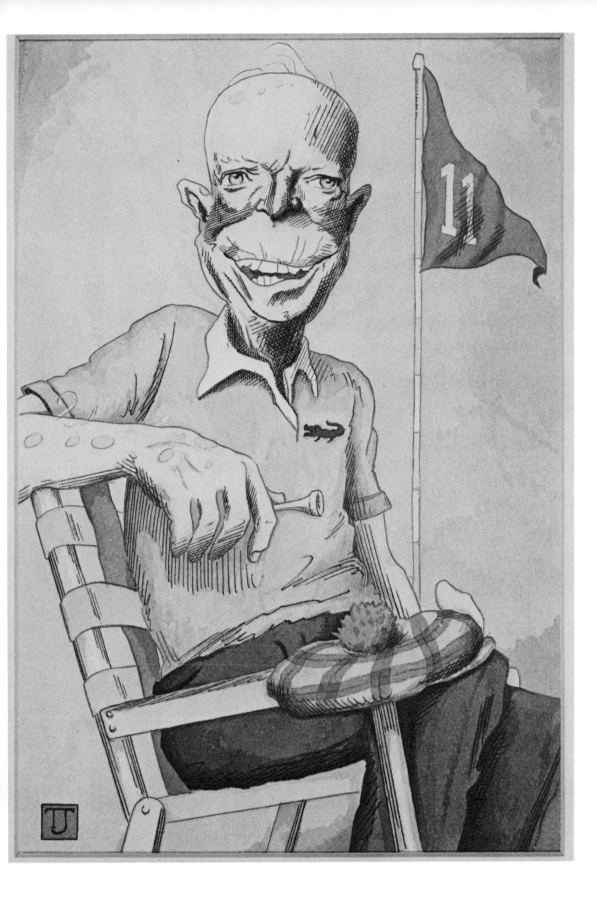

John F. Kennedy   1961-1963

John was born in a manger in Brookline, Mass.
Or was it the castle of the ruling class?

His sovereignty started with words so true:
"Ask not what your country can do for you"

From Berlin until Cuba the people did sing
Of the charm and glory of the once and future king

Perhaps, though, my memory misbehaves
Wasn't it Lincoln who freed the slaves?

I picture Hyannisport, but my mind's out of order
Or is that really JFK walking on the water?

Lyndon B. Johnson   1963-1969

This species of American bird
Despite its looking rather absurd

Had grit and cunning and a powerful beak
To peck the rich while protecting the meek

Tough and quick and legislatively nimble
It was for a time our national symbol

Until, that is, it horribly bungled
When released into a Vietnam jungle

Such foul habitat was not meant for a turkey
The foliage too thick, the rivers too murky

When finally withdrawn, its wings were clipped
It died back in Texas, where it had been shipped

Richard Nixon   1969-1974

The Nixon years, if put to song:
Confused lyrics of right and wrong

Indeed few eras can proclaim
So much of both sacred and profane

Revenue sharing, that trip to Peking
Of such success, we praise must sing

Then killing of four college chums
Who, after all, were only "bums"

As Christmas bombs fell on Hanoi
Kissinger brought tides of joy

There is no further reason to argue
It's *nolo contendere* for Spiro Agnew

The music fades, the voices blur
A tape recorder starts to whirr

But before the music is complete
It stops abruptly, does not repeat

Rosemary reaches for her wrap
She moves her foot and leaves a gap

Gerald Ford   1974-1977

Nixon's chopper departed, but begging your pardon
Wasn't that Jerry who just tripped in the garden?

Yes it was—look, there's Betty; now she's taking his arm
Gee, I hope the new president has met with no harm

Buttering muffins next day, he's rather a boaster:
"Tomorrow I'll remember to plug in the toaster!"

But the thing about Ford that stays on to amaze
Is how memory tells us—ah, those were the days!

Jimmy Carter   1977-1981

James Earl Carter hailed from the South
A few too many teeth in his mouth

During winter he wore a cardigan sweater
Perhaps some day we'll understand him better

He made us a promise never to lie
But look into his rattlesnake eyes

As Commander-in-Chief he was man of the hour
But Jimmy Carter never understood power

The result was that Jimmy lost some respect
Old Brezhnev thought him a total reject

His brother provided him grand entertainment
Till Billy signed on as a Libyan Agent

At Carter's legislation the Congress balked
While at his ego Teddy mocked

In the foreign arena he made his last stand
There trapped by mullahs in Iran's shifting sand

Ronald Reagan   1981-

Conservatives, mounting a sixteen-year quest
Clinched the election for their man from out West

Retired matinee champ, peddling borax and Barry
Surprised all the pundits, forty-four states to carry

Armed with branding-iron, Bible and fixed bayonet
A Messiah to save us from our National Debt

So bleeding hearts, Bella and Bonzo beware
The actor now sits in the director's chair

He's funding his movie through the private sector
A comedy starring his budget director:

The flick's got suspense, lots of laughs, some romance
In one scene Mr. Stockman swipes Tip O'Neill's pants!

Tip strides to the podium, calls Stockman a "louse"
But his bare spindly legs simply bring down the House!

The scene cuts to Haig, who is cautioning Moscow
In trenchcoat, speaking oddly, like Inspector Clouseau

It's a box office smash that folks crowd in to see
Not bad for a movie that's just rated "B"

Add-Monitions

George Washington   1789-1797

"...with teeth made of wood"

Sets of Washington's false teeth were made from all sorts of material, including lead. A set of wooden dentures, to my knowledge, has never been found. His teeth were causing him acute discomfort in 1796, when he sat for Gilbert Stuart, and Stuart's famous portrait reflects a man suffering in quiet dignity. In January 1797, Washington wrote his dentist complaining of "gaps" and "loose spots," or with words to that effect. Today, of course, our leaders smile as they pose for official portraits. Mr. President, it seems, has become "Mr. Polident." For more about teeth see Jimmy Carter.

John Adams   1797-1801

"His Rotundity"

John Adams was short and squat and generally disliked. But pompous and unpleasant as he might have been to his political associates, John and First Lady Abigail exchanged delightful correspondence for years. Late in life Adams began writing long thoughtful letters to Jefferson. According to legend Adams' last utterance—he died on the same day as Jefferson: July 4, 1826—was "Thomas Jefferson survives!" Whether or not the story is true (U.S. Grant's final remark, a desperate "Water!", was not profound but more believable), Mr. Adams was incorrect, as Mr. Jefferson had died several hours earlier.

Thomas Jefferson   1801-1809

"Be it Barbary pirates..."

Libyan-American relations have long been strained. The United States waged its first war against North African pirates and the unscrupulous beys of Tripoli who financed them. And it was during this war at sea that swashbuckling Stephen Decatur declared, "Our country, right or wrong!"

"...mud streets and mosquitos..."

Early Washington, D.C., was a swamp: no paved streets, snakes falling out of newly planted trees, the town turning to soup during heavy rains. Government buildings were difficult to erect on the marshy grounds Congress eventually purchased for the city. The "original" Washington Monument, its cornerstone laid in 1848, sank.

"...bathrobe and slippers"

Jefferson loved to lounge while he worked. The Commander-in-Chief would receive congressmen and foreign dignitaries still dressed in his fur-collared bathrobe and wearing slippers. When Ronald Reagan was governor of California he conducted much of his nighttime office work in pyjamas. For another lounger-in-chief see Chester Alan Arthur.

James Madison   1809-1817

"Jemmy"

. . . was his nickname. Madison was our smallest president: five foot four, one hundred pounds or less, in spite of all the ice cream First Lady Dolley served him.

While gasping his last, by the way, in 1836, he was reported to have squeaked, "I always talk better lying down."

James Monroe   1817-1825

"Era of Very Good Feelings"

Not everyone was so jolly. An elector named Plumer, from Vermont, voted for John Quincy Adams in 1820. He said only George Washington deserved election by acclamation. Everyone else voted for Monroe.

John Quincy Adams   1825-1829

"He forged a deal with Henry Clay"

In the election of 1824, Adams finished second, electorally and popularly, to Andrew Jackson. Henry Clay and William Crawford also received electoral votes, enough to deny anyone a majority. In the House of Representatives, Clay threw his support to Adams, which action decided the election. Adams then made Clay his secretary of state. "A corrupt bargain!" Jacksonians howled, bringing an end to the "Era of Good Feelings." Jackson retaliated by launching his 1828 presidential campaign early.

Long, tiring campaigns are not a new feature of American politics. William Henry Harrison didn't really stop running after he was beaten in 1836. The Lincoln-Douglas debates in the Illinois senate race in 1858 were an obvious warm-up for both candidates. Teddy Roosevelt's Bull Moose campaign and Jimmy Carter's quest lasted two years or more. But the modern record, set by Ronald Reagan, should hold for many years. Official or unofficial, on and off again, his campaign(s) can be traced back to 1968, or maybe 1964.

"...his icy stare"

Like father, like son: John Quincy Adams was cold and detached. He said so himself: "I am a man of reserve, cold, austere and forbidding manners. My political adversaries say a gloomy misanthrope; my personal enemies an unsocial savage. With the knowledge of the actual defects of my character, I have not the pliability to reform it . . ."

Andrew Jackson   1829-1837

"Second Bank of the United States"

. . . of which Nicholas Biddle was chairman. Jackson wasn't enamored of banks: "I hate ragg tagg banks and empty pockets."

"To the victor, the spoils"

New York Senator William L. Marcy made this remark as he defended Jackson's appointment of Martin Van Buren as ambassador to Great Britain. Jackson's party apparatus, the first of its kind in America and perhaps the world, took Marcy's remark seriously. It remains the essential philosophy of machine politics. Jackson's hordes gathered on the White House lawn on Inauguration Day, 1829, to celebrate as they waited for political hand-outs. This blatant job-seeking practice survived through many administrations, dying out at the turn of the twentieth century and the progressive era of Theodore Roosevelt.

Martin Van Buren   1837-1841

"...little red Dutchman from up Sleepy Hollow"

Martin Van Buren, alias the "Red Fox of Kinderhook" and "The Little Magician," grew up in the very Dutch Hudson Valley, setting for many Washington Irving stories.

William Henry Harrison   1841

". ..minus hat, coat or tails"

Harrison, sixty-eight years old when inaugurated, was no picture of health and had surpassed the average lifespan long before then. Now the legend has many versions, but roughly they all go like this: Conscious of being an old man, Harrison wanted to demonstrate his virility before the common folk. So he delivered his address, the longest and surely the most boring in history, coatless and hatless in a cold drizzle. He remained scantily dressed all day, galloping about Washington on a horse. He coughed and wheezed himself to sleep that night, and one month later he was dead.

Harrison might have survived had his doctors left him alone. While still a young man, Harrison had apprenticed briefly to a doctor. Throughout his life he had treated most of his ailments himself, principally those of an intestinal nature (he had horrible indigestion). But now as president he let the experts take over. He was diagnosed as suffering from pneumonia, so they lacerated one side of him, using stinging ointments and suction cups. Later, when he was in a weakened condition and complaining of intestinal cramps, his doctors administered strong cathartics. The combination finished him off.

John Tyler   1841-1845

"It was 'Tyler Too' who set precedent"

Succession was not clearly defined in the Constitution. Originally, losing candidates for the presidency were then elected vice-president. In 1840 Harrison chose Tyler, a Democrat, to be his running-mate—a fatal mistake! Because Tyler was not a Whig, and because he chose to assert his powers, Henry Clay, and therefore Congress, could not control his presidency. John Tyler deserves a higher ranking among our presidents than he normally gets. The unwritten laws of succession, firmly established by Tyler, have not since been seriously questioned.

94

James K. Polk   1845-1849

"Amazing, what he managed to do"

Polk, the first dark-horse president, was the last powerful president be-fore Abraham Lincoln. Between 1845 and 1861, the United States fell apart at the seams over slavery. The famed dark horses, by the way, have a poor track record on Election Day. I can think of only three others who were elected to the presidency: Franklin Pierce, Warren Harding and Jimmy Carter. And two of those may not genuinely qualify. Harding wasn't an unknown, but merely the product of backroom brokering. And Jimmy Who?, of the early 1976 primaries, marched triumphantly into Madison Square Garden, his nomination sewn up on the first ballot. George McGovern, Wendell Wilkie, John Davis, James Cox and Alton Parker, who all perhaps qualify for the dark-horse category, were not so lucky. William Jennings Bryan, a surprise in 1896, went on to lose three times.

Zachary Taylor   1849-1850

"From the Halls of Montezuma ... to the Stores of Taco Bell"

My memory fails me here. Either the Mexican War inspired this military hymn, or it was written before the war, and actually *sung* by American soldiers as they marched to Veracruz. Group singing was a favorite pas-time of Americans back then, from battle songs to campaign songs.

At age sixty-four, Taylor cast his first vote in an election . . . for himself . . . for president, in 1848.

Millard Fillmore   1850-1853

"What did you do?"

For further information write: The Millard Fillmore Museum
                                   24 Shearer Ave.
                                   East Aurora, N.Y. 14052

Franklin Pierce   1853-1857

"In Sectional tangles..."

The war between slave-owners and "Free-Soilers" in the Kansas Territory was the most glaring of sectional squabbles between North and South. Pierce's difficulties were compounded by emotional tragedy and alcoholism. Two months before the inauguration, Pierce and his wife saw their only surviving son crushed to death in a train accident. Two months later Mrs. Fillmore died, and in April, Pierce's vice-president Rufus King died. Jane Pierce, who had never approved of her husband's political career, remained secluded in a White House bedroom for nearly half his term. For the remainder of her life she was believed never to have smiled. Franklin Pierce, incidentally, was considered among the handsomest men of his day. How tastes change.

James Buchanan   1857-1861

"Our grand Constitution..."

Buchanan was a scholar of constitutional law. The Constitution was a convenient document behind which he could hide. He much preferred learned debate to resolution. Heaven forbid should the losing team go home mad, or the victory celebration disturb the decorum.

Abraham Lincoln   1861-1865

"...in the shape of a smile"

And who could keep one? A smile, that is. Lincoln was the first president to sit regularly for photographers. And a grave chore it must have been. The negatives took forever to develop. All the lanky fellow could do was sit there. An uncontrolled emotional outburst, such as a smile, would have registered as a blur before the camera. So the hundreds of photographs of Lincoln are all quite serious. Of course the times were tough. But Lincoln was a legendary teller of tales, a champion jokester. Political cartoonists of the time depicted him as not taking the war or Congress seriously enough. "That reminds me of a little joke," captions often began. We'll never know about Lincoln's smile. Perhaps he showed a lot of gums. For more about gums see Jimmy Carter.

Andrew Johnson   1865-1869

"...mending old breeches"

Young Andy Johnson was apprenticed to a tailor. He opened a tailor's shop in Greenville, Tennessee, before entering politics. Johnson, elected

96

to the Senate in 1856, remained there after Tennessee seceded. In 1862 Lincoln appointed him military governor of the state, and two years later chose Johnson as his running-mate on a "unity" ticket. But Northern Radicals, firmly in control of Congress after Lincoln's death, sought vengeance. They held Johnson, a Southern Democrat, in contempt, sabotaging his reconstruction plan and later impeaching him.

Ulysses S. Grant   1869-1877

"...penning memoirs"

Grant's memoirs are considered the best writing by an ex-president. Of course Gerald Ford is still sharpening his pencils.

Rutherford B. Hayes   1877-1881

"While the First Lady served lemonade..."

"Lemonade Lucy" Hayes, an avowed advocate of temperance, served no alcohol in the White House. The lawns were kept better, too, I'm sure, as the constant parade of office seekers marched elsewhere to cool off.

James A. Garfield   1881

"...odd stunts or juggling"

I first learned that Garfield liked to relieve the day's tension by standing on his head from a "facts 'n' trivia" strip in the Sunday comics. This tidbit of information was later confirmed on the back of a cereal box.

Chester Alan Arthur   1881-1885

"...set a most royal routine"

Garfield's running-mate loved to slap backs in the backrooms of New York's political establishments. He'd acquired a sleazy reputation as collector of the Port of New York. But upon becoming president he abandoned his old ways, in style as well as substance. He ignored his old cronies, championed civil service reform to their chagrin, and acquired the look of a dandy. He became a fashion-plate, swished the wine in his mouth before swallowing it, and cultivated the company of snobs.

Grover Cleveland   1885-1889; 1893-1897

"For White House style cooking..."

He loathed it: "I wish it was to eat a pickled herring, a Swiss cheese and a chop at Louis's instead of the French stuff I shall find." I imagine it was an entire herring, too. And perhaps a second pork chop. Only Taft outweighed Cleveland.

Benjamin Harrison   1889-1893

"...there must be a few"

Like Rutherford Hayes and John Quincy Adams before him, Harrison's election was only an electoral victory, and perhaps his principal accomplishment at that. Grover Cleveland clipped him by 100,000 votes. Although not overtly fraudulent, Harrison wrongly called his election an act of Providence. "Harrison would never learn," Pennsylvania GOP boss Matt Quay confided, "how close a number of men were compelled to approach the gates of the penitentiary to make him president . . ."

William McKinley   1897-1901

"...the Gilded Age"

. . . a phrase coined by Mark Twain and Charles Dudley Warner, title for their novel of the U.S. Grant era. Historian Robert Kelley calls it, "a time of hypocrisy, shallow glitter, dollar chasing, and political irresponsibility." Sounds like the Sunbelt.

Theodore Roosevelt   1901-1909

"...twixt antelope and anteaters"

T.R. may have practiced conservation on a grand scale, but on safari he rarely practiced restraint. He always shot his limit, which was usually the sky. His home, Sagamore Hill, is a monument to taxidermy. A favorite chair of his is in fact a gaudy assemblage of antelope antlers. At least he put the fruits of his victories to constructive use.

Some credit for this poem belongs to Stefan Lorant, author of *The Presidency: A Pictorial History of Presidential Elections from Washington to Truman.* In a chapter on Roosevelt's first term, he presents the following extract from a poem published in an English weekly magazine:

> A smack of Lord Cromer, Jeff Davis a touch of him
> A little of Lincoln, but not very much of him
> Kitchener, Bismark and Germany's Will
> Jupiter, Chamberlain, Buffalo Bill

William Howard Taft   1909-1913

"All four hundred pounds..."

Taft never tipped the scales beyond 332 pounds. But he seems to have gained stature over the years.

Woodrow Wilson   1913-1921

"He'd teach Fourteen Points..."

Americans generally have rejected the intellectual in favor of the pragmatic approach to politics. Wilson barnstormed the country, attempting to instruct his constituents in the value of joining the League of Nations. Everywhere he was met by audiences of hostile America-Firsters. The Senate rejected the Treaty of Versailles, and Wilson, his health ruined by the tour, suffered a stroke. Wilson remained secluded in the White House, mostly bedridden. First Lady Edith Galt Wilson, in those hushed times, took over some of the nominal functions of government and maybe more.

Warren G. Harding   1921-1923

"...Florence stalks the halls in a huff"

Their relationship resembled that between Margaret Dumont and Groucho Marx. Florence stalked Warren Harding all across Marion, Ohio. The courtship was Flossie's effort, her handsome beau succumbing meekly. They were married over her father Amos Kling's objections. Kling, a wealthy local banker, despised the Hardings and their politics.

He believed them to be Negroes and said so. (This charge was hurled at Harding throughout his career. In the 1920 presidential election, an Ohio college professor published and circulated a pamphlet "documenting" Harding's Negro ancestry. His broad nose, substantial lips and slightly olive complexion were dead giveaways, some thought.*) Florence pursued her husband as though he were her career. She nurtured his political ambitions, supplying the self-confidence he lacked. She dismissed the whispers about his extracurricular activities. Shortly after he died, as the stories of scandals and lurid affairs began to break, she burned much of his private correspondence. Florence Harding died in 1924, her work complete.

*William Howard Taft also endured rumors that he was really a mulatto, partly because of his appearance and partly because he was fond of dining with servants in the White House kitchen.

Calvin Coolidge   1923-1929

"...his thought for the day"

A picture's worth a thousand words. The stoic Yankee knew how to manipulate the news media. He was perhaps the first president to don funny hats and engage in presidential "clowning," however silent it may have been. While vacationing in Vermont, for instance, Coolidge would pretend to be a farmer. Slipping into clean overalls, his shoes polished, he'd pose with his scythe—a good Republican publicity shot. Closer inspection of one farming photo even reveals his presidential limousine parked in the background.

Chief Executive clowning may have reached a nadir with Jimmy Carter, who, while touring Mississippi river towns aboard the Delta Queen, once put on a Groucho Marx disguise and imitated the comedian's walk. The show got mixed reviews.

Herbert Hoover   1929-1933

"...his garage and his chickens"

A campaign slogan of Hoover's was, "A car in every garage, and a chicken in every pot," to combat the threat of encroaching Depression.

Through the administrations of Harding and Coolidge, Herbert Hoover served as secretary of commerce and "under-secretary of everything else." Mining engineer, food administrator in Europe after World War I,

100

chairman of many a task force, Hoover became our first and only bureaucrat president.

Franklin D. Roosevelt 1933-1945

"...you're a tough act to Fala"

Roosevelt's longtime companion was his black Scottie Fala. In 1944, Republicans attacked Fala for being a nuisance and extravagance. The specific charge was that Roosevelt had left Fala behind on the Aleutian Islands, and then sent a destroyer back to retrieve him. Fala resented these smears, Roosevelt asserted: ". . . His Scotch soul was furious. He has not been the same dog since." It was one of his most successful speeches of the '44 campaign. He beat Dewey that November by three million votes.

Among dog-owning presidents, Warren Harding was perhaps the most devoted. Dogs may have been Harding's only true friends. He wrote editorials about them in the *Marion* (Ohio) *Star* and considered these the best examples of his writing. Evidence suggests that two of his dogs, Jumbo and Hub, were poisoned at the behest of rival editors. He wrote of Hub:

> ". . . One honest look from Hub's trusting eyes was worth a
> hundred lying greetings from such inhuman beings, though they
> wore the habiliment of men."

Harding's last best friend was his Airedale Laddie-Boy. As Harding's administration began to crumble, a famous show-business dog "wrote" to Laddie-Boy, offering moral support for his master. Laddie-Boy returned a thank-you note, with Harding's guiding hand. The president signed the letter "Laddie-Boy." A statue of the beloved dog, donated by the Newsboys Association in honor of the president, was placed in the Smithsonian Institution.

Harry S. Truman 1945-1953

"...inscribed on my tie"

Large, loud ties were fashionable in the late forties . . . as were double-breasted jackets and very broad lapels. Perhaps it was one last fling at flamboyance before the onset of the suspicious, conspiratorial 1950s. But pleasantly embroidered profanity ties, like the one Mr. Truman is wearing, didn't attain popularity until the early seventies, when for a time they were hot items in novelty shops.

Dwight Eisenhower   1953-1961

"...funny guys in sweatshirts and sneakers"

Beatniks, of course. Sweatshirt and sneakers were the uniform, plus a goatee if you could grow one, a la Maynard G. Krebs.

John F. Kennedy   1961-1963

"Of the charm and glory of the once and future king"

Kennedy knew the television eye was watching him in 1960, and he was prepared. He practiced poise and mastered it. Not so, Nixon. During the Great Debates, Kennedy, a cum laude graduate of charm school, sat relaxed in his chair while Nixon squirmed. (Since then, political debaters have mostly stood behind podiums carefully adjusted to compensate for discrepancies in height and weight.) Kennedy even learned how not to sound tired. He hired a speech therapist who taught him to orate resonantly from his diaphragm, in the manner of an opera singer.

Much has been made of the importance of the West Virginia primary to Kennedy's election in 1960. West Virginia, a bastion of Fundamentalism, was considered the supreme test for a Catholic. In the primary Kennedy defeated a Protestant and longtime friend of West Virginians, Hubert Humphrey.

Forgotten is the fact that in 1928, Al Smith, the first Catholic candidate for president, won the West Virginia primary. His opponent was Senator James Reed of Missouri, an ordained minister.

Lyndon B. Johnson   1963-1969

"It died back in Texas..."

In the four years of Johnson's retirement, he never reemerged as a spokesman for his party. Mostly he remained on his ranch, enjoying the luxury of turning in early for bed and sleeping undisturbed until morning. The Democrats, still reeling after the '68 convention and election, purged LBJ from their memories. Four years later, in Miami, it was as though Johnson had never existed. And again the Democrats cut themselves in two over Vietnam. (A common political occurrence, forgetting the past: Nixon's name has not been invoked in the past two Republican conventions. And Jimmy Carter is once again "Jimmy Who?")

Lyndon Johnson did what some old retired politicians do, though. He let his hair grow, at least in the back. The whitish mane that swept up over his collar was first revealed to millions when George McGovern met Johnson at his ranch for an obligatory handshake and a lukewarm blessing in 1972.

Richard Nixon   1969-1974

"...bums"

Speaking of bums, which is how Richard Nixon described campus protestors of the Cambodia invasion, the president suffered terribly from "five o'clock shadow." Nixon was not blessed like Kennedy with handsomeness. The shadow gave him a sinister appearance, which cartoonists duly recorded. After the 1968 election, Herblock, of the *Washington Post*, portrayed Nixon in a barber shop, having just received a "clean shave" from the cartoonist. But the shadow soon returned. Nixon's unfortunate sweat glands further prevented him from turning television to his advantage. Under the glare of television lights a pool of perspiration would form above his upper lip and glisten. Smaller puddles of the salty solution would appear below his dark darting eyes. Now and then a bead of sweat was seen to ski down his nose and hang there on the cliff for a while before dropping off. Not the best defense for a president on the witness stand during ruthless press conferences.

Gerald Ford   1974-1977

"...who just tripped in the garden"

Among Ford's more memorable falls:

6/1/75—Salzburg, Austria: The president slipped and fell several rungs while deplaning Air Force One. A military aide and Austrian Chancellor Bruno Kreisky got him back on his feet.

12/26/75—Vail, Colorado: Ford took a spill in a morning ski run with members of the U.S. Olympic ski team.

5/7/76—Washington: The president bumped his head while negotiating the doorway of his presidential helicopter parked on the White House lawn.

6/25/77—Milwaukee, Wisconsin: "I'm very sorry," the former president told a spectator at the Vince Lombardi Golf Tournament, after whacking him with a drive on the first hole. The man survived.

"Buttering muffins next day..."

Perhaps it was just plain old toast. But Gerald Ford showed he was just plain old folks when he buttered his morning toast before TV and newspaper cameramen. And plain old folks was right, too. Gerald Ford was plain-spoken and plain-featured. Why even his first dog, a Boston terrier, was named "Spot."

Jimmy Carter   1977-1981

"...too many teeth in his mouth"

That, plus a general oral malaise, hurt Carter's effectiveness in presenting his programs. His failure to enunciate made for dismal speechgiving. Yet during press conferences or at some of the smaller "town meetings," when his voice could be heard above the din, Carter was at his best. He answered questions thoughtfully, his syntax and grammar the best that's been heard from the East Room in years.

"...his rattlesnake eyes"

The impassive steely eyes belied his constant smile. Set in a blotchy complexion, they sometimes suggested a reptilian gaze and caution.

Ronald Reagan   1981-

"The actor now sits in the director's chair"

Ronald Reagan now directs from his chair in the Oval Office. But who sat in the director's chair on the set of "Bedtime for Bonzo"?
Clue: "Here's Johnny!"